The Princess and the Pea

Once upon a time, there was a king who had only one son. The king loved his son dearly and was worried about him. His son had reached the marriageable age.

"The problem is not in choosing a good wife for you," said the king. "There are hundreds of princesses with beauty and brains."

"Then what are you worried about, Father?" asked the prince.

"Most of the princesses are not real princesses," explained the king. "Their blood is not pure royal blood. And in our family, we have always married real princesses only."

"Well, if that's all that's bothering you, don't worry," smiled the young man. "I'm sure I can find a real princess. I'll leave today and begin my search."

And so it was that the prince set out with high hopes. He rode a splendid stallion with a golden mane. Soon, he crossed the border of the small kingdom where he was born and entered the neighbouring country of Silvania.

The king and queen of Silvania were delighted to meet the prince. They had heard rumours that he was seeking a bride, and so they lost no time in introducing their daughter to him. She was a young girl with sad eyes and a pale complexion.

"You'll be staying for a few days, I suppose," the king asked the prince.

"Perhaps," the prince replied. "But first, tell me if your daughter is a true princess of royal blood?"

"Oh, yes," said the king. "That is . . . well, practically. All her family, except her grandmother, are of royal lineage."

"Who was her grandmother?" asked the prince.

"Well, she was the queen's maid," replied the king reluctantly.

The prince hid his disappointment, but he soon left. He could not marry the granddaughter of a servant!

In each kingdom he visited, disappointment greeted the prince. One princess had too big a nose, one was fat, one had frizzy hair, and one had a whiny voice. But more important, none was a real princess!

For six months the prince travelled, trying to find a true princess whom he could marry. But he did not meet even one princess who was a real princess. Finally, the prince gave up and returned home.

The king and queen were sad to see their son return without a bride. They became sadder yet when they saw how lonely he was.

Months passed, and though they continued to search, they still could not find a real princess. "Maybe we shouldn't insist that her blood be absolutely pure," said the king. "If she is beautiful and intelligent, wouldn't that be enough?"

"No," said the queen. "Our family has never settled for less."

"But if our son never marries, there will be no more family!"

"The right girl will come along. We just have to wait," said the queen.

The next winter was very hard.
It rained without stopping, and gusts
of wind tore branches from the trees.
The prince never left the palace.
He moped about, wondering
if he'd ever find a bride.

Late one night, he sat yawning over a book of
poetry, watching the rain trickle down the window
panes. Suddenly, there was a loud knock on the door.

The servants had gone to bed. So the prince answered the door himself. A beautiful young girl stood outside. She was elegantly dressed, but her clothes were soaked through.

"Excuse me for bothering you," she said, "but I got lost in the nearby woods."

Her golden hair hung limp from the rain, and her whole body was shivering with cold. The prince gazed into her crystal blue eyes and fell head over heels in love with her.

"Who are you?" he asked.

"The Princess of Sustrom," she said. "We were crossing the woods when my carriage overturned. The coachman got badly hurt, and my maid fainted. So I decided to look for help and got lost in the storm."

"Come right in," said the prince. Then he called the servants, and sent them to find the carriage and to help the coachman and maid.

"This is the girl I want to marry!" he said aside to the king and queen.

"We shall see," said the king. The king, the queen and the prince met the supposed Princess of Sustrom over a late-night snack.

"You have been so kind to me," said the princess.

"It is nothing," said the king. "Merely our duty."
He looked the girl over carefully. " I don't think I know your country. Is Sustrom far from here?"

The princess described her country, which was nestled far away in the mountains. She answered all the other questions the king put to her. Eventually, the king was convinced that she was a real princess. The prince had been convinced long before. He was so in love with the girl that he had forgotten to eat. But the queen was not so easily convinced. She decided to test the girl.

"It would be foolish to try to travel in this bad weather," the queen said to the princess. "I will have a room prepared for you."

The princess accepted, and the queen went quickly to the guest chamber. She ordered the mattress to be removed from the bed. She took a small pea and placed it in the middle of the bed, and ordered twenty of the softest mattresses to be placed on top of the pea. Each mattress was stuffed with the softest goose feathers.

"We shall see what happens!" smiled the queen when the princess climbed into the bed.

Next morning, the queen went to greet the princess. "How did you sleep last night?" she asked the young girl.

"I hate to say so, but I had a terrible night," replied the princess, looking exhausted. "I couldn't sleep a wink, I was so uncomfortable. There was something hard under the mattress. I tried to avoid it but it stuck into me like a knife. My body is covered with bruises!"

The queen smiled with satisfaction. No one but a real princess could have noticed the presence of a single pea under twenty mattresses. Only a true princess of royal blood could have such delicate skin!

The prince was anxious to hear his parents' decision about the young princess.

When the queen kissed her son good morning, she whispered in his ear, "If this young lady is to your liking, go ahead and ask her to marry you. She is a real princess. There can be no doubt."

The prince ran to the princess to declare his love for her. The princess also lost no time in confessing that she had also fallen in love with him.

The wedding was held the following spring, and it is said that few royal couples have been happier. The pea, which brought such happiness to the newlyweds, became one of the most valued treasures of that country.

If anyone doubts that this story is true, let him go to a small kingdom up north in the mountains, where everyone's favourite food is peas.